With the help of the ancient science of Numerology, you can determine your future and find solutions to all your problems.

Dr. Shrimali tells you all about numbers, their significance, characteristics, alphabets, elements, planets, gems, parts of body, directions, countries, towns, dates, days, months, professions, relationships, calculation of numbers that influence you, planet figures, relative periods, sub-periods, forecast for the year, month, day, hour, minute, interaction of names and numbers, and correction of spellings for a better future.

The author of this book is the famous astrologer, Dr. Narayandutta Shrimali, whose predictions have come true time and again.

Other books

- A Handbook of Palmistry
- Cheiro Book of Numbers
- Cheiro Language of Hand
- Bejan Daruwalla's
  Annual Horoscope
- Bejan Daruwalla's
  Love Signs

Numerology
Made Easy

Numerology
Made Easy

Dr. Narayandutta Shrimali

HIND POCKET BOOKS

NUMEROLOGY MADE EASY
© All Rights Reserved
First Paperback Edition, 1965
This Paperback Edition, January 2009
ISBN 81-216-0263-7

Published by
Hind Pocket Books Pvt. Ltd.
J-40, Jorbagh Lane, New Delhi-110003
Tel: 24620063, 24621011 • Fax: 24645795
or Post Box No. 3005, Lodhi Road Post Office, New Delhi-110003
E-mail: fullcircle@vsnl.com • *website:* www.atfullcircle.com

Printed at Dot Security Press Pvt. Ltd, New Delhi-110028

PRINTED IN INDIA
65/09/02/01/21/SCANSET/DSP/DSP/DSP

Contents

Introduction

Numerology is easily the most ancient science in the world. Its origin is in India and the rishis, prophets of old, used to predict the future accurately by it.

It is important for a proper study of the science of numerology to have concentration and a balanced mind. A little mistake results in wrong results. Numerology is a secret science — a secret in which the good and the bad, the future and the past of a man is hidden. The whole universe is a result of a combination of five basic elements, viz., water, fire, air, earth and ether. Man is affected by these elements and has a link with the world.

Mantras are composed of 32, 24 or 12 words, a clear indication of the importance of numbers. In fact, words and numbers possess an intimate and mutual link.

The Indian rishis had given due importance to numbers from 1 to 9, besides the *shoonya* (zero). With the help of these they had formulated a formidable system of mathematics. These numbers possess latent secrets which have not been fully explored yet. Numbers have a specific history. They have their functions and importance. It is essential to understand the specific characteristics of numbers.

According to these rishis, each number symbolises a specific characteristic and order. Man cannot be freed from the family of numbers. In the real sense, numbers can be called friends of a person and share his joys and sorrows.

For example, a person's date of birth is 25 April, 1940. Then the number 25 has assumed an indissoluble part in his life. This number 25 will not only be liked by himself but also by his wife, brothers, friends, relatives and associates. On this very date, the individual will experience that his enthusiasm, courage and energy have been strong. Not only this, every moment of his life will be measured and tested through the science of numbers. When did you marry? When were you blessed with a son? When did you pass your examination? All the indelible marks of life will be exhibited through these numbers. Emerson has rightly said that without numbers there is no existence. Our whole life is configured by numbers. The basis of every event of our life lies in numbers. Thus, it is definite that whatever we want to do or can do is through numbers. Whatever we do or wherever we go, numbers go with us and remain with us throughout life.

Numbers possess a specific order, a specific speed and a specific function. Unless a person concentrates, he cannot understand these characteristics of numbers. Our whole life is determined according to a fixed plan of numbers.

Lets us take the example of Adolf Hitler. He was born in 1889. His year of birth dominated his whole life.

Example

Year of Hitler's birth:

$1 + 8 + 8 + 9 = 26$

When this number 26 is added to 1889, we get 1915, when an important work of his life, the writing of his autobiography, *Mein Kamph*, was completed.

Year 1915

  + 1

    9

    1

    5
    ——

Year 1931 — the year of the birth of the Nazi Party.

  + 1

    9

    3

    1
    ——

Year 1945 — the year of the death of Hitler.

You will notice that in the life of Hitler, there has been a definite and significant order of number 2.

1. Birth: 20 April = 2 + 0 = 2

2. The first meeting of Nazi party:
    24-11-1920
    2 + 4 + 1 + 1 + 1 + 9 + 2 + 0
    Total 20 = 2 + 0 = 2

3. Oath of Allegiance to the
    German Constitution:
    = 21-2-1932
    2 + 1 + 2 + 1 + 9 + 3 + 2
    Total 20 = 2 + 0 = 2

4. Became Chancellor on 30-1-1933:
    3 + 0 + 1 + 1 + 9 + 3 + 3
    Total 20 = 2 + 0 = 2

5. Recognition of the Nazi party on
    1-12-1933:
    1 + 1 + 2 + 1 + 9 + 3 + 3
    Total 20 = 2 + 0 = 2

6. Locarno Treaty:
    7-3-1936
    7 + 3 + 1 + 9 + 3 + 6
    Total 29 = 2 + 9 = 11 = 1 + 1 = 2

7. Czech Invasion:
    13-3-1939
    1 + 3 + 3 + 1 + 9 + 3 + 9
    Total 29 = 2 + 9 = 11 = 1 + 1 = 2

8. Signing of the Treaty of Surrender:
    22-3-1939
    2 + 2 + 3 + 1 + 9 + 3 + 9
    Total 29 = 2 + 9 = 11 = 1 + 1 = 2

Thus, readers can notice the influence of number 2 on the whole life of Hitler.

Example

Napoleon Bonaparte was also influenced by numbers:

   1769 — Year of birth of Napoleon

   + 1

      7

      6

      9
   ─────
   1792 — Year of the revolution

All these events clearly depict that the life of man is continuously influenced by numbers. These numbers possess a definite speed. If only an event or two are established, the same can be attributed to coincidence. But when the incidents in a person's life occur in regular order, we cannot resist the conclusion that numbers positively have some significant secret.

America is the most powerful and most wealthy nation of the world. Number 4 governs her. The important events in the history of America linked with number 4 reveal this fact.

1. Date of birth of first President, George Washington:
   22 Feb. $(2 + 2 = 4) = 4$

2. Declaration of Independence:
   4 July = 4

3. Order of Civil War:
   13 April $(1 + 3 = 4) = 4$

4. Fall of the Fort:
   13 April $(1 + 3 = 4) = 4$

5. Battle of Donaldson Fort:

13 Feb (1 + 3 = 4) = 4

6. Battle of Fredricks:
   13 Dec (1 + 3 = 4) = 4

7. Victory of Manila:
   13 Aug (1 + 3 = 4) = 4

8. President Wilson's visit to France:
   13 Dec (1 + 3 = 4) = 4

9. Use of Fleet in the First World War:
   13 June (1 + 3 = 4) = 4

10. Decisive Battle of St. Mitchell.
    13 Sept. (1 + 3 = 4) = 4

11. Death of President Jefferson who
    declared Liberty:
    4 July = 4

12. Death of President Munro:
    4 July = 4

13. Number of pieces in the American Flag:
    13 (1 + 3 = 4) = 4

14. Number of stars over the eagle in the Flag:
    13 (1 + 3 = 4) = 4

15. Stripes in the American Flag:
    13 (1 + 3 = 4) = 4

16. To the moon — Apollo 13:
    13 (1 + 3 = 4) = 4

17. The number of States in America
    at the time of Independence:
    13 (1 + 3 = 4) = 4

The above events show that America was under the influence of numbers 4 and 13. Most of the important historic events in America were either influenced by number 4 or by number 13.

Astrology and palmistry are as difficult subjects as numerology is easy. Readers are advised that they should write out the main events of their lives in a chronological order. They will notice that a certain number is influencing them. It has its say in every important event of their life. Note that a particular number and you, will see that your future will be governed and influenced by it. If you do this life will become easier and happier.

1
Numerology

Numerology has the basic importance of the first 2 digits or numbers from 1 to 9 which are termed as root numbers. The numbers after 9 are added together and thus reduced to least numbers. The maximum number of days in a month in an English calendar is 31. The method of deduction relates to numbers up to 31. For example, if a person is born on the 18th, the root number for 18 is 9 (1 plus 8 equals 9).

Number		Root Number
1	—	1
2	—	2
3	—	3
4	—	4

Number		Root Number
5	–	5
6	–	6
7	–	7
8	–	8
9	–	9
10	1 + 0	1
11	1 + 1	2
12	1 + 2	3
13	1 + 3	4
14	1 + 4	5
15	1 + 5	6
16	1 + 6	7
17	1 + 7	8
18	1 + 8	9
19	1 + 9 = 10 = 1 + 0	1
20	2 + 0	2
21	2 + 1	3
22	2 + 2	4

Number		Root Number
23	2 + 3	5
24	2 + 4	6
25	2 + 5	7
26	2 + 6	8
27	2 + 7	9
28	2 + 9 = 10 = 1 + 0	1
29	2 + 9 = 11 = 1 + 1	2
30	3 + 0	3
31	3 + 1	4

Similarly, in the manner indicated above, we can deduce the least number or root number of a number exceeding 31.

While taking into consideration the effect of numbers, only the date of birth of the person is to be taken and the least number deduced. The month and year of the person should not be taken, since only the least number of the date of birth of the individual is effective.

2
Significance of Numbers

Every number or digit has its own significance and importance. Persons influenced by a particular number possess all those properties which that number has. By number we mean the least number or root number. For example, if a person is born on 2nd August, he will be influenced by the properties of number 2. Similarly, for persons born on 23rd April, number (2 + 3 = 5) 5 would influence them. The month and year are not given importance. The characteristics of each number are given below:

Shoonya

Shoonya, zero or cypher, is an indication of the universe. This digit never appears independently. When it appears with any other digit, it increases by tenfold the value of that digit. This digit is a pointer towards perfection. When this digit is associated with the life of an individual, that individual is considered to posses self-determination, wisdom and can be fully relied upon. The individual neither tries to do a wrong thing nor advises others to do so. Persons associated with *shoonya* are generally self-centred. Persons born on the tenth, twentieth or thirtieth of a month are affected by the digit *shoonya* and believe in frankness.

One

Number 1 is an indication of high, best or chief. Persons with 1 as their root number are born to march ahead. Their power of forbearance is excellent. They face terrible ups and downs in life but they keep courage and do not become frustrated or accept defeat.

They possess a strong disposition for leadership. They provide leadership to their companions and friends at an early age and to their colleagues in advanced age. No slackness in their leadership can be visualised. They sacrifice for the upliftment of their friends. They share their joys and sorrows and offer all needed assistance even in their hard times. This is an inborn trait of theirs.

A person with digit 1 has a wide circle of acquaintances. It is one of their special traits to make friends easily with strangers in a short time and maintain everlasting friendship with them. They are trustworthy and helpful. Society admires their actions and qualities. Their friends have blind faith in them and are always ready to do anything for them.

Persons having 1 as their least or root number are always on the lookout for new things in life. They do not admire the beaten track. They believe in doing the job in a better way. It is their trait to do something new which when presented is always admired. Such people leave some new legacy for posterity.

Their physical constitution is strong and robust. They possess a good physique and mental balance. Such people, successful in the performance of jobs of a physical nature, do not lag behind in their mental ability and in exercising good judgement.

In business and services, they will be leaders. Their success lies in their far-sightedness, with the result that they would be able to achieve much in a comparatively short time. In whatever field they are, they do not rest on their oars till they achieve their aims. They command many persons under them and their leadership coupled with far-sightedness will be in evidence.

Such persons have a distinct goal before them. They remain fully alive to their goal and steadily march towards it. They neither grope in the dark nor encourage anybody else to do so. Such people are clever in taking decisions. A clear and to-the-point reply, appropriate to the time and place, is their speciality. Indecision is nominal in their life. Their ability to take a quick decision in any work or business constitutes the secret of their success. Such a decision is generally right. Whatever decision they take, they stick to it and after taking the decision, they neither change it nor repent it. An independent personality, an independent decision and an independent life — these are their specialities. They do not work under threat and pressure from anybody. They are the architects of their own thoughts which are backed by their own experience, wisdom and far-sightedness. Such people are very successful in their lives.

Two

Number 2 is a representation of perfection. It indicates that any kind of work which is undertaken should be interesting, systematic and perfect in itself.

People with 2 as their least or root number are not generally of a sound physical constitution, but mentally they are healthier and stronger. Compared to physical vocation, they possess more affinity towards a vocation which results in the creation of works for the masses who remain indebted to them for ages to come.

Such people are very sentimental. They very happily attend to the work of others. They are seldom capable of saying 'No' to anyone. Being kind by nature, they believe in sacrificing for others.

They possess a refined taste in beauty. They are more capable of understanding love and beauty in greater depth than others. They know the art of infatuating others. They can make acquaintances in a very short time. They do not hesitate at all in confessing their mistakes. They lack self-confidence and are often caught in arguments with their own selves. They frequently change their thoughts in accordance with the advice of their friends. By virtue of their gentle and straight-forward nature, they are prone to exploitation. Even when aware that persons approaching them seek their own selfish ends by flattery, such people keep mum.

They are more imaginative which makes them sensitive. Mental turmoil goes on within them. Due to impatience, they take wrong decisions and later continue repenting when they do not achieve the desired results. Pessimism and an inferiority complex hold them and they feel sad and insulted. Even though they have a good number of friends, most of them are selfish. They will feel the absence of real friends and cannot remain friendless for long. Their friends do take advantage of them but they neither reciprocate nor mind it.

They possess a natural tendency to read the minds of others. The opposite person may speak or may not speak out anything, still they are able to penetrate his mind and measure its depth. Their interest in fine arts takes much of their time and energy. They will have the privilege of having charming, sober and educated spouses. Their married life is usually normal. They are sentimental, broad-minded, helpful and brainy.

Three

Number 3 is said to be the most favourable and best of all digits. It contains all those characteristics possessed by root numbers 1 and 2. Persons with the root number 3 are quite courageous, bold and are capable of completing the job they have undertaken.

They can express their feelings and thoughts better than others. They can influence others by their polished and diplomatic behaviour. They can even convince those unacqainted with them of their views and make them favourably inclined towards themselves.

Though financial hardships stand in their way, they achieve their aims by hard work and struggle. They do not get disheartened or disgruntled easily in life. They stick to their decisions and once they adopt a path, they do so with firmness.

Their expenses are high. They spend particularly on luxury items, articles of enjoyment and decoration. They do not think before taking a decision while spending money.

They entertain high ambitions. A small position, small work and a little money do not attract them. They rise slowly but steadily in the financial field.

They feel frustrated when they do not achieve their objectives. This frustration lasts a short time and then they work with more vigour and zeal till they succeed.

Though they always think of a sudden rise or sudden pecuniary gains, such events are very rare in their life. They progress steadily and attain stability.

They do not benefit to an appreciable extent from their family or brothers but still they remain ever ready to help them. Their success is entirely due to their own efforts.

They insist on carrying out their own ideas. For this reason, although they are not quarrelsome, they succeed in making more enemies and creating a rift between them and their friends.

They are always engrossed in their work. They do not like to remain idle. They neither interfere in the affairs of others nor do they like others interfering in their affairs. They are liberal-minded and willing to lead a clean and simple life. They do not believe in show business.

They get angry quickly. But their anger melts away as quickly as it comes. Even though they are hot-headed, they do not allow wisdom and discretion to leave them.

They influence the persons around them. They are capable of shattering the views of others and dominating them. They possess the special characteristics of turning a foe into a friend. Though they have many friends, they will not get help from them.

Number 3 is a symbol of sex. Even though they strive hard in the field of love, they do not succeed. They do reap some benefits but they miss final success by a narrow margin. Their spouses will usually be charming, chaste, loyal and contribute much to the happiness of family life.

Their childhood is not free from hurdles and impediments but during their youth they are able to surmount them and this makes their future life happy and cheerful.

There are travels in their life. They not only benefit from the journeys they undertake but their zeal is also enhanced. In the matter of discipline, they are hard and exacting. They desire that their families and subordinates should also be disciplined like them.

Persons with root number 3 command respect. They achieve their aim in some particular field.

Four

Persons with 4 as their root number have continuous ups and downs and struggles in life. Such people strive hard to attain stability in life but their efforts are negated due to the environment taking unfavourable turns. It is unthinkable that they will be able to accomplish anything, howsoever small or big, without opposition or obstacles. They advance in life but only after surmounting considerable ups and downs.

Such persons have a cool temperament but when angry, they tend to forget everything. Personal loss is often suffered by them as a result of such anger. But their anger goes away as quickly as it comes. When their anger is gone, they are regretful and feel sad at the self-invited loss.

They are sober and tolerant by nature. Their friends and relatives regard them as simple and honest and hence take undue advantage of them. Even then they tolerate it knowingly.

Suddenness is a peculiar characteristic of their life. They try to proceed by organised planning but do not succeed due to the sudden rising of unfavourable circumstances. They are compelled to make quick changes in their plans and accomplish their work.

Although their life is full of ups and downs, struggles and labour, they advance in life from time to time. They may often take advantage of such ups and downs.

Nothing positive can be said about their temperament, thoughts and policies. They plan a thing in the morning and make a fundamental change in it in the evening. Their opponents get defeated on this very point.

They are broad-minded and very clear at heart. They do not conspire against others. They are plain-speaking, which sometimes pinches others, with the result the latter feel insulted, though this is usually not the case.

They keep things and matters to themselves and are capable of keeping secrets.

There is no dearth of enemies for them. If you defeat one enemy, five more will crop up. Their enemies conspire behind their backs and do their worst in creating difficulties for them but fail miserably. Thus, the enemies can create hurdles and nuisance for them but cannot harm them ultimately.

They know the art of making friends. They will make sacrifices for their friends but later realise that either their friends have betrayed them or are not reciprocating the help rendered. They suffer more from friends and relatives than from strangers and enemies.

Although they exercise due care and take precautions before undertaking any work, they are instrumental in such actions which turn sour or unfavourable to them in future and result in loss.

They are incapable of taking quick decisions. They think for hours together on a problem but are unable to reach any conclusion. They work and act on the advice of friends and intimate persons.

At times they feel sad and isolated. They feel lonely and think that there is no one to help them.

Sudden material gains in their life do not exist. Whatever they have to achieve is by the dint of their hard work and struggle. Thus, they should not associate themselves with gambling, lottery, etc.

Though they do not spend unnecessarily, their expenditure is beyond their means; they should have control over this. This surprises people and keeps them in suspense.

They are unduly quick and intolerant. They desire that everything should be done without loss of time, with the result they take some actions without necessary thinking and consideration.

Their family life will be congenial but their spouses will be weak in health. They are likely to suffer from heart trouble in old age, for which they must take all precautions in anticipation.

They will not enjoy the blessings of their father for long. They will not benefit much from their brothers and relatives. In their youth they will meet with difficulties in securing a job of their liking. They will face obstacles in their academic career.

They are open-minded. If they have money they spend it lavishly with the result that they always feel acute shortage of finance.

If they want to progress, they must learn to say 'No' to others and should not make false promises. This will add to their prestige.

With age, their prestige, financial condition and status will enhance.

Five

Number 5 is considered to be an important digit in

numerology. The greatest characteristics of persons with this number is that they posses a knack of winning over others. After a very short time, they are able to make the other person turn in favour of their point of view. Not only this, with their behaviour, honesty and clear heart, they establish their position in the minds of others and succeed in striking everlasting friendships.

Such persons remain awfully busy in their life. They know the value of time and how best to utilise it. Travels are ingrained in their very nature and they derive much pleasure from them. But due to their preoccupations, they rarely travel. But it is certain that every travel works to their advantage.

They are mentally very strong. They are quick in taking decisions. Whatever decision they take will prove advantageous to them in future. They cannot physically exert much, but they do not tire of mental work.

Their greatest quality is to mould themselves to fit any situation. They are innocent children in the company of children, revolutionary youths with the youth and mature men in the company of old people. Thus, they command respect in every walk of life and their opinions are given due weightage.

They are often spendthrifts and can spend too much at times. Before spending, they think many times and once the expenditure increases, they are capable of controlling it.

Their aptitude for accomplishing work is commendable. The moment any new idea or plan comes to their mind, they engage themselves in it wholeheartedly. They do not rest till they achieve their aim.

They detest any plodding kind of work and seem naturally to drift into all methods of making a fast buck. They possess a keen sense of earning money with new ideas. They cannot sit idle, because their nature is to be up and about.

Generally, such persons are business or trade-oriented. They use their minds to find how best profits can be made from the work. Although they have to face many hurdles, they do not yield. They continue with the same energy and zeal with which they started till they succeed in their mission. People with root number 5 who are in service can be more successful if they engage themselves in a side-business. They have chances of getting sudden financial gains. They should buy lottery tickets, etc.

They are prepared to take risks in life — this is an innate trait in them. Only they can succeed in life who take risks. They get opportunities, correctly assess the situation and mould themselves accordingly. Their capacity to adapt themselves according to time, place and situation is quite significant. These two qualities make them attain high positions in life.

They inevitably have someone to help them always. If one helper has turned his back on them, another takes his place.

They have an inclination to learn new things and have new ideas in life. They do not take much time to grasp difficult work and soon become experts. They cannot concentrate on one job for long. In between, they change their line. This drawback in them compels them to change their plans, with the result that they cannot attain perfection in any single field.

They make friends easily and maintain their friendships till their last breath. Friends are their wealth and share their joys and sorrows of life. Friends contribute much to their progress.

Persons with number 5 endeavour to live with dignity and accomplish all their aims in life.

Six

Number 6 is most impressive and the best digit of numerology. The most beautiful women and handsome men on earth are linked with this number. They are symmertical, attractive and possess refined tastes. They dress nicely, in a most pleasant way, so as to be always in presentable shape. They hate disorder, dirtiness, ugliness and mismanagement. They are materialistic and believe in a comfortable and luxurious life.

In spite of lack of adequate finance, they spend freely where they feel the urge to spend. They like to do work of an artistic nature which is unique. Such persons are very popular among the public. They are able to extract top secret information from others by their diplomacy and cleverness. They are successful in achieving their goals easily.

They are always smiling and cheerful. They are never seen under distress. They have characteristics of pleasing persons, among whom they find themselves, by their talk, jokes and make the gathering full of fun and happiness.

They do not lead a normal married life. Even though they have a spouse living, they have intimacy with others of the opposite sex. They respect others' sentiments but remain puzzled due to experiencing weakness in them. Their bent of mind towards others' love creates an upheaval in their married life which appears smooth only superficially and externally.

They are emotional by nature. They cannot concentrate on one subject nor can they sit in one place for long. They prefer field-work which requires travelling.

Women with 6 as their root number are first to start a new fashion. They are not only in the front row in fashion, but they are also foremost in arranging items of luxury at home. Even though they may be financially hard up, they maintain themselves so nicely that others cannot suspect the truth.

Their living place is attractive and fully equipped with gadgets of modern comfort. They like wearing white clothes which greatly add to their personality. A smile is their invaluable wealth which turns an enemy into a friend.

They have a pivotal position in society. They are good mixers but no one can easily guess their inner secrets. What is up their sleeves the next moment cannot be guessed even by their close friends. They cannot remain alone. This is their weakness. They always want a companion. A feeling of despair soon overtakes them. Any action not to their taste makes them frustrated and they try to get rid of that despair at the earliest. Their affection, love and cooperation makes them popular in society.

Seven

Root number 7 is prominent in compassion and cooperation. Poets and philosophers are influenced by this number. They are lucky that they are controlled and influenced by this number.

Their brain is fertile and active with new plans. They do not consider anything useless. They have the calibre to put everything to advantage.

They achieve splendid success if they take interest in creative work. Their writing has originality and their thinking has refinement which attracts others and bonds them with their views.

Obstructions and hurdles come in their way; yet they succeed in their aim by making concerted efforts. Undoubtedly, they are bold and courageous. They do not leave a job till it is accomplished.

Whatever they have achieved in their life is purely due to their own efforts. There is very little contribution from their brothers and relatives even to their own elevation. With regard to their family environment and circumstances, they will notice that they have crossed many a milestone which an ordinary person is incapable of doing.

Their main mark is their originality. They do not adopt the beaten track but do their job in a fashion which reflects originality and refinement. Things which are considered useless by others can be put to some use or other by them, which makes them attractive.

Their second strong point is power of independent thinking. They neither remain nor keep anybody under duress. They possess a strong will to take independent decisions. Though they do take advice from their acquaintances, they weigh all the pros and cons and then take a decision. Taking the counsel of others has the advantage of giving them the benefit of thinking of others and to what length a particular person can be of help to them. Thus they are able to decide the likely result of an action under execution. Thus, no planning of theirs goes haywire. Their third prominent point is their broad individuality. They do not pay attention to small jobs. They always undertake important work. They take precautions while doing any work so as to dissuade others to cast aspersions on their personality. They do not pay attention to trivial mistakes of their servants. Their field of acquaintances is wide. Their behaviour is refined. They know the art of extracting work from others. They possess full zeal and energy to elevate themselves in life.

In society they are looked upon with respect. Though they are busy most of the time, they devote some of their time to social activities. They continue to hold an important place in society by virtue of their prudence, temperament and work.

They are never satisfied in their life, with the result they are always active and progressive. They mould themselves appropriately to the changing environment.

They possess a wonderful intuition to know the mind of a person with whom they may happen to be talking. This is one of their special characteristics.

They possess a very good memory. They get full cooperation from their friends and also reciprocate it. They struggle for their friends' upliftment. Even though some of the friends deceive them, they do not retaliate in the same manner even though they are annoyed. This is an extraordinary quality in them. They take interest in undertaking big tasks. From their childhood, they have a strong desire to travel abroad. With their intensive efforts, they go abroad many times in their lifetime. Their married life is normal but can be made happier with effort and diplomacy. It can be said with certainty that their life is happy and prosperous.

Eight

Number 8 represents upheaval, revolution, anarchy, waywardness and eccentricities of all kinds. Persons with this number cannot sit down at ease. Though such people have the ability and are ready to make concerted efforts to progress in their life, they have to conquer unaccountable problems and hurdles before they accomplish their goals.

They are of a meditative nature. They go on with their work without much fun. Whenever their work is accomplished and comes to the notice of the public, people cannot refrain from paying tribute. Working like this is their special trait and generally they are known to have magnetic attraction.

They are grave by nature. They do not like exaggeration or anything of low taste. They are never satisfied with small deeds. They do not undertake any work which they find unfavourable. Whatever they say is based on solid proof and on the solid foundation of experience. People regard their word as trustworthy and authoritative.

Their speciality is that they do not easily spell out their secret. Whatever they are going to do the next moment is beyond the thinking not only of others but even of their nearest relatives and friends.

Whatever events take place in their lives are sudden and indifferent. Their lives are full of ups and downs and terrible struggles but even then they know how to live. People will be wonderstruck to see their progress through struggles. Even though there is turbulence in their mind it is not reflected on their faces. Thus, it is difficult to understand them.

They are friends in need but at the same time they are bitter enemies of their foes. They are ever ready to sacrifice anything for the sake of their friends. They will even suffer a loss and undergo hardship but will not allow any harm to come to their friends. They do not hesitate to crush a person who is their enemy or who deceives them. To shatter the evil designs of enemies is a characteristic of their mind but they do not come out in the open. A middling situation is absent in their life. Either the gain is of a very high order from the work they undertake or they suffer heavily from it.

They are stiff outwardly but are very soft within. Though they appear like a rock, they have a flowerlike tender heart. They have no intention to harm anybody. They render help to the extent they can. Making jokes, gossiping or whiling away time is simply unthinkable and intolerable for them. It is their endeavour to attain the highest position with full honours in society.

It is a strong characteristic of their personality that they remain cheerful even under stress and strain. They possess flexibility which makes them withstand many shocks. Thus they are always happy and cheerful.

Their lives are motivated by service. They serve with a pure motive people in distress, the sick and the worried. That service will have neither any artificiality nor show about it nor any intention of self-advertisement. Their weakness is that they are materialistic for which they remain ever ready to sacrifice anything. They consider wealth to be the ultimate end and objective of life. Whatever their endeavour in life, whatever their labour, its root will always be in wealth. They are not opposed to service but they are definite that they can flourish only through business.

They have very little interest in religious matters. They consider saints as hypocrites. There is no hypocrisy in their life nor are there any great moments of amusement in their life. Once they undertake any work, they do not rest till it is accomplished. They feel dejected if the work is not done to their taste and satisfaction. They are always gripped by false doubts and fears, with the result that they proceed with too many precautions. To have an unnecessary argument or a quarrel with anybody erodes their happiness. Addiction and vice are their weaknesses. Any slight relaxation of control brings them failure.

Nine

Number 9 is the most powerful, and a strong number. Its representative planet is Mars, which believes in kill or be killed. It cannot brook defeat or insult. People with number 9 shine in the world and are prepared to die for their honour. They do not hesitate to undertake the most difficult task and by their grit, strong will and determination, succeed in their mission.

People with this number are daring, both physically and mentally. But their daring sometimes goes to extremes and results in tragedy. However, this does not deter them. They possess courage, boldness, self-determination, resolve and the ability to lead, from their birth.

Persons with number 9 are so brave that they perform wonderful and astonishing deeds. Such people appear to be aggressive externally but are indeed soft-hearted from inside. They are austere and well-disciplined but at heart they are compassionate and even generous. Though they are capable of establishing standards of discipline, they are popular with their subordinates. They do not hesitate to take responsibility for making the most adamant of persons yield. They are capable of creating situations by which they extract the work and complete it according to schedule.

They are impulsive by nature. They become turbulent over trifles and adopt an opposing attitude. Persons with number 9 do not give much importance to officials, which results in a rift between them and the officials.

Their married life is normal. Rift with spouse may result. Sometimes they suspect their spouses and are on the lookout to find their weaknesses. They chide them in public which spells uncertainty in married life.

They get involved in some lawsuits or quarrels. Neither do they remain calm nor allow others to have peace of mind. They cannot remain uninvolved in incidents of suffering. They are advised to control their minds and act judiciously without haste.

They have more than one person in their lives which sometimes defames them in society. Due to this, they have at times to face financial hardships. Wine and intoxicants become a habit in their youth. Even though knowing the bad effects of vice, they will not be able to control themselves. This can prove harmful and disquieting. Also false pride, showing off, window-dressing are all present in them, and consequently they suffer.

Hurry is the weakness of their character. When someone speaks, they give their verdict without even fully hearing him. This haste gives rise to many awkward situations for them. To get annoyed over trifles or show enthusiasm and haste is not in their favour. Their friends can be counted easily. Sometimes their behaviour makes their friends into enemies.

Persons with number 9 as their root number are proud and self-righteous. They work their way through obstacles and adversities. They do not beg from others and do not yield. They do not lose heart. Their fundamental principle of life is to push forward. They dash on constantly and rest only when they accomplish their mission. In field-work, they exhibit their wonderful ability for organisation. They possess a peculiar characteristic of togetherness. There is a firmness in their speech which attracts persons who come in contact with them. By virtue of their personality and hard work, such persons attain a prestigious position in society.

3
Numbers
and Their
Characteristics

In this chapter, I will discuss the facts relating to numbers.

1. Numbers and Their Related Signs

Number	Planet/Sign
1	Leo
2	Cancer
3	Sagittarius
4	Aquarius
5	Gemini, Virgo
6	Taurus, Libra
7	Pisces
8	Capricorn
9	Aries, Scorpio

2. Numbers and Their Related Letters

Number	Planet/Sign
1	A, J, S
2	B, K, T
3	C, L, U
4	D, M, V

Number	Planet / Sign
5	E, N, W
6	O, F, X
7	G, P, Y
8	H, Q, Z
9	I, R

3. Numbers and Their Related Elements

Number	Element	Characteristic
1	Fire	Godly
2	Water	Emotional
3	Fire	Godly
4	Air	Mental
5	Air	Mental
6	Earth	Practical
7	Water	Emotional
8	Earth	Practical
9	Fire	Godly

4.   Numbers and Parts of Body

Number	Parts of Body
1	Forehead, Brain
2	Heart, Lungs, Chest, Throat
3	Thighs, Feet
4	Calf, Heel, Jaw
5	Neck, Hands, Breath, Nose, Height
6	Face, Eyes, Nose, Tongue, Bones
7	Blood
8	Ankle
9	Hair, Sexual Organs, Urine

5.   Numbers and Gems

Number	Gem	Colours
1	Ruby	Pink and Orange
2	Pearl	White, Cream, Blue
3	Topaz	Yellow and Green
4	Sardonyx	Coloured

Number	Gem	Colours
5	Emerald	Green and Black
6	Diamond	White, Blue
7	Cat's eye	Pink, Yellow, Green
8	Sapphire	Black, Green
9	Coral	Red, Yellow

6. Numbers and Directions

Number	Direction
1	East
2	North-West Angle
3	North-East Angle
4	East
5	North
6	South-East Angle
7	North-West Angle
8	West
9	South

7. Numbers and Professions

1. Work related to Electricity, Surgery, Ambassadorship, Science, Research, Leadership, Captainship, Ships, Jewellery.

2. Liquids, Travel, Hotel, Journalism, Music, Dance, Poetry, Work relating to Land, Ice, Silver, Dairy, Agriculture, Animals, etc.

3. Teaching Service, Judicial Service, Civil Service, Ambassadorship, Philosophy, Police, Law, Banking, Advertisement Work.

4. Railways, Aircraft, Mining, Technical Work, Stenography, Tailoring, Clerical, Lecturing, Engineering, Architecture, Astrology, Magic, Archaeology, etc.

5. Engineering, Sales, Accounts, Law, Railways, Telegraph, Journalism, Tobacco, Radio, Commission Agency, Insurance, Writing, Editing, Transport, Politics, Mental Work.

6. Architecture, Engineering, Jewellery, Foreign Currency, Food Inspection, Hotel Production, Music, Literature, Watch Repair, Social Work, Fine Arts, Scents and Perfumes, Flowers, etc.

7. Films, Travel, Dairy Farm, Driving, Secret Service, Fish Selling, Medicines, Hospital, Liquids, C.I.D., Archaeology, Wrestling, Rubber, etc.

8. Games, Engineering, Police, Mayoralty, Heavy Weight Lifting, Municipal Works, Contracts, Tobacco, Law, Gardening, Music, Mining, Poultry, Jail, Labour, etc.

9. General Leadership, Command, Work Relating to Fire, Medicine, Banking, Work Relating to Machinery, Religious Work, etc.

8. Numbers and Their Related Days

Number	Day
1	Sunday
2	Monday
3	Thursday
4	Saturday
5	Wednesday
6	Friday
7	Thursday
8	Saturday
9	Tuesday

9. Numbers and Their Related Countries and Towns

Number	Countries and Towns
1	India, Pakistan, Turkey, Burma, Afghanistan, Hong Kong
2	London, Tibet, France, Germany, Sri Lanka, Delhi, Kabul, Portugal, Ethiopia
3	England, Nepal, Cambodia, Holland, Australia, New York, Denmark, Bhutan
4	Italy, Washington, Kuwait, Bombay, Hungary
5	Korea, Saudia Arabia, Singapore, Spain, America, Goa, Allahabad
6	Canada, Russia, Czechoslovakia, Japan, Berlin, New Zealand
7	Kashmir, Greece, Moscow, Scotland, Rhodesia, Bangkok, Sweden
8	China, Peking, Austria, Addis Ababa
9	Indonesia, Calcutta, Paris, Sikkim

10. Numbers and Favourable Dates

Number	Dates
1	1, 3, 5, 7, 10, 11, 12, 14, 16, 19, 21, 23, 25, 28
2	2, 4, 6, 9, 11, 13, 15, 20, 22, 24, 26, 31
3	1, 3, 5, 7, 9, 10, 12, 14, 21, 23, 27, 30
4	2, 4, 6, 8, 9, 11, 13, 17, 20, 22, 26, 29, 31
5	1, 4, 5, 7, 8, 10, 12, 16, 19, 23, 28
6	2, 4, 6, 9, 15, 18, 20, 22, 24, 29
7	1, 3, 5, 7, 8, 9, 10, 14, 16, 19, 23, 24, 29
8	3, 5, 7, 8, 12, 13, 16, 17, 21, 23, 25, 30
9	1, 2, 3, 4, 6, 7, 9, 11, 13, 15, 19, 20, 21, 28, 29, 30

11. Numbers and Favourable Days

Number	Days
1	Sunday, Wednesday, Thursday
2	Monday, Tuesday, Friday
3	Sunday, Tuesday, Thursday
4	Monday, Tuesday, Friday
5	Sunday, Thursday, Saturday
6	Monday, Tuesday, Friday
7	Sunday, Monday, Wednesday, Thursday
8	Thursday, Saturday
9	Monday, Tuesday, Thursday, Friday

12. Numbers and Months

Number	Months
1	January, March, May, July, September, October, December
2	April, September, November
3	March, May, July, September, October, December
4	February, April, June, August, September, November
5	January, March, May, July, August, October, December
6	February, April, June, November
7	January, March, May, August, September, October
8	January, March, April, May, August, December
9	February, March, April, June, July, September, November, December

13. Numbers and Friends

Number	Fast Friends	Friends	Neutral	Enemy	Bitterest Enemy
1	2, 7	5	3, 9, 4	6	8
2	5	6, 3, 8	1, 4	7, 9	–
3	2, 7, 9	8	1, 4	–	6, 5
4	2, 7	5	3, 9	1, 6	8
5	1, 4	3	2, 7, 6	9, 8	–
6	–	3	2, 7, 1, 4, 5,8	9	–
7	5	6, 3, 8	1, 4	2, 9	–
8	–	3	2, 7, 9, 5, 6	–	1, 4
9	–	8	1, 4, 2, 7, 3	6	5

14. Relationship of a Number with Other Numbers in its Period

For Number 1

1 Gainful but unnecessary worries and more expenses

2 Sudden gains, success in work

3 Weak health, unnecessary expenditure, difficulties

4 Obstructions, mental agonies

5 Gainful

6 Opposing environments, obstructions

7 Most favourable, auspicious and financial gains

8 Health deterioration, loss, litigation, worries

9 Normal gains

For Number 2

1 Normal gains

2 Unnecessary worries and pain

3 Favourable news, gains

4 Success with difficulties

5 Sudden financial gains, success in work

6 Respect, progress, financial gains, favourable news

7 Health deteriorates, hurdles

8 Gainful

9 Many more difficulties, debts and worries

For Number 3

1 Ordinarily favourable

2 Special financial gains, success in business

3 Ordinarily favourable

4 Normal

5 Most painful and harmful

6 Deceit, loan, loss, disease

7 Gainful

8 Auspicious work

9 Unexpected financial gains

For Number 4

1   Harmful, worries

2   Most gainful

3   Success with difficulties

4   Normal

5   Favourable news or gains

6   Harmful, pain, disease

7   Special financial gains

8   Loss, loan, disease

9   Normal

For Number 5

1   Special gains

2   Generally troublesome

3   Favourable and good news

4   Success in work and monetary gains

5   Normal

6   Favourable news

7   Success with difficulties

8   Malignment, defamation, painful, financial
     loss

9   Theft, difficulties, worries

For Number 6

1   Ordinary gains

2   Favourable

3   Special gains

4   Success with difficulties

5   Obstructions

6   Favourable

7   Normal

8   Auspicious news

9   Sudden financial gain, difficulties

For Number 7

1   Ordinary gains

2   Disease, pain, loan

3   Favourable

4   Success with difficulties

5   Special gains

6   Favourable

7   Normal

8   Financial gains

9   Painful, worries

For Number 8

1   Most harmful, financial loss and obstructions

2   Ordinary gains

3   Most favourable news

4   Loss, problems and worries

5   Ordinary life

6   Success with obstructions

7   Gainful

8   Normal

9   Most favourable and auspicious news

For Number 9

1 Normal

2 Success with obstacles

3 Ordinary gains

4 Favourable

5 Most painful and worries

6 Disease, loan and loss

7 Ordinary gains

8 Sudden financial gains and augmentation of business

9 Normal

4
Numbers and The Future

In Indian astrology, there are basically nine planets —Sun, Moon, Mars, Mercury, Jupiter, Venus, Saturn, Rahu and Ketu. Every planet has its own individual number which it represents. I give below the planets and their related numbers:

Sun	:	1
Moon	:	2
Jupiter	:	3
Rahu	:	4
Mercury	:	5
Venus	:	6
Ketu	:	7
Saturn	:	8
Mars	:	9

To know the future with the help of the numbers draw four horizontal and four vertical lines, thus making a figure comprising 9 parts which is called 'Janma Kundali' or horoscope. The position of the 9 planets is shown in these nine parts. In the horoscope given below, each part represents a fixed position for a planet.

5	3	7
6	1	8
2	9	4

To understand this figure, prudence and perseverance are required. The central portion is fixed for the Sun. The number related to the Sun is 1 and in the centre 1 is written. Likewise, there are three rows, each representing three planets.

Mercury — Jupiter — Ketu   : First Row

Venus   — Sun   — Saturn : Second Row

Moon   — Mars   — Rahu   : Third Row

This position of the planets is fixed. The first row represents mental strength, the second represents physical strength and the third row spiritual power.

For predictions, the date of birth is considered. According to the system accepted all over the world, the date changes at 12 o'clock at midnight. From the date of birth to the making of a horoscope or figure of planets, the following facts should be kept in view:

1. For the figure of the planets, the date of birth should be considered.

2. In the date of birth, the numbers of the century are not taken into account. For example, if somebody's birth-date is 21-4-1935, only 21-4-35 will be counted. In the year there is no necessity to write 19.

3. If the number in the date of birth is repeated twice, then that number should be counted once only. For example, if someone was born on 25-4-40, here the number 4 has been used twice. But while making the figure, number 4 will be considered once only.

4. Zero is not taken into account.

5. The characteristics of each number are given on the facing page:

Number	Characteristics
1	Personal freedom, pride, ego, personality
2	Change, kindness, love, travel
3	Wisdom, knowledge, understanding, learning, money
4	Economy, lottery, practicability, pride, supervising capacity
5	Cleverness, wisdom, fine intellect, language, science, mathematical knowledge
6	Art, music, painting, beauty, literature, social eminence, love
7	Effect, prominence, progress, courage, physical power
8	Corruption, disease, death, loss, hunting, accident
9	Freedom, cleverness, fire, risk, superiority

Now, I will explain the method of making a planetary table date-of-birth-wise. If a person is born on 21-4-35, the figure will be as given below:

5	3	
	1	
2		4

From this birth-figure or planet-figure, the following facts are clear:

1   Date of Birth: 21-4-35

2   Sum total: 2 + 1 + 4 + 3 + 5 = 1 + 5 = 6

3   Planet relation: Mercury — Jupiter

First row: Jupiter — Sun

4   Planet relation: Mercury — Moon

Second row: Moon — Rahu

Note — Those numbers which are nearer to each other, the relations of these numbers or planets are known as of first level. If there is a gap between the two numbers but they are in a single line, then that relation is of second level.

The relation of planets of first level is more effective on the life of an individual.

Predictions

In this planet-figure, there are two planet relations of first level, Mercury — Jupiter and Jupiter — Sun.

Mercury — Jupiter

Mercury imparts cleverness, wisdom, intellect, and at the same time is responsible for learning and providing money. Thus the person's earnings are based on the planet Jupiter. With education and teaching, he will have materialistic gains and succeed in achieving respect in society.

Jupiter — Sun

Sun is the main planet for personal freedom. Jupiter is for wisdom and knowledge. Thus, this person will rise in society due to his knowledge and wisdom and will simultaneously make himself important.

Mercury — Moon

In this planet-figure, the relationship of Mercury-Moon is of second level. Mercury represents wisdom. Moon represents kindness and love. Thus, the person is kind and looks after the welfare of others in his life. He will never harm anybody. Due to high integrity, he will attain an important place in society.

Moon — Rahu

This relation is also of second level in the planet-figure. Moon imparts kindness and love. Rahu imparts supervising capacity and etiquette. He will make wise plans and achieve success.

Details

The sum-total of the date of birth was 6 which is represented by Venus. Thus the person will be fully influenced by the characteristics possessed by Venus. He will take keen interest in the fields of art, music and social behaviour. In his life when he is in the period of Venus, he will progress.

Number 6 will have much importance for him. The years 6, 15, 24, 33, 42, 51 and 60 are important years because the sum-total of the years is 6. Similarly the dates 6, 15, 24 in every month will be most favourable, gainful and progressive for him.

Numbers 2, 4, 6 and 9 are friends of number 6. Thus such dates will also be favourable. Most incidents in his life will take place on these dates. The century whose root number is 6 will also be favourable.

Numbers 1, 3, 5, 7 and 8 are inimical to number 6. Thus as far as possible, no important work may be initiated on these dates.

Number 6 is representative of the planet Venus. Thus white clothes will be favourable in the progress of the individual. Now, I will explain for the benefit of readers, the planet-figure of a few persons.

Bhagwati Devi

8-4-33

	3	
		8
		4

Total = 18 = 9
Planet Relation: Saturn — Rahu

Nand Kishore

16-12-55

5		
6	1	
2		

Total = 20 = 2

Planet Relation: Mercury — Venus

Venus — Moon

Venus — Sun

Kailash Chander

18-1-58

5		
	1	8

Total = 23 = 5

Planet Relation: Sun — Saturn

Saroj

30-1-61

	3	
6	1	

Total = 11 = 2

Planet Relation: Venus — Sun
Jupiter — Sun

Arvind Kumar

4-7-67

		7
6		
		4

Total = 24 = 6
Planet Relation: First level — 0
Second level: Ketu — Rahu

Nirmala Kumari

8-9-69

6		8
	9	

Total = 32 = 5

Planet Relation: Second level: Venus — Saturn

Rajendra Mal

4-3-37

	3	7
		4

Total = 17 = 8

Planet Relation: Jupiter — Ketu

Anil

21-5-62

5		
6	1	
2		

Total = 16 = 7

Planet Relation: Mercury — Venus

Venus — Moon

Venus — Sun

Note — Readers should make the planet-figure with the help of the date of birth and find out the effect of various planet relationships and also the number which is more effective in an individual's life.

5
Planet-Figure
and Period

After making the planet-figure, a study of the main-period and sub-period of a number, under whose influence at present you are, may be made.

For this, it is essential to go into minute details. Thus, a note of your date of birth and time of birth is made. The periods of each planet and its related number are given on the facing page:

Planet	Number	Years
Sun	1	6
Moon	2	10
Mars	9	7
Mercury	5	17
Jupiter	3	16
Venus	6	20
Saturn	8	19
Rahu	4	18
Ketu	7	7

Method

Total all the numbers of the date of birth. The numbers of the century should not be counted. For example, if someone was born in 1940, then only 40 should be taken while totalling the numbers.

Find the root number of the total. The main-period of that number will start at the time of the birth.

For example, if a person was born on 21-4-35, then $2 + 1 + 4 + 3 + 5 = 15 = 1 + 5 = 6$. So, root number is 6 which is related to Venus. Thus, at the time of birth, the person was in the main-period of Venus, whose duration is 20 years.

Now, the remainder of the main-period of Venus at the time of birth is to be found out. For this, the time of birth should be known.

In the foregoing example, the person was born on 21-4-35 at 9.50 a.m. The counting is started from 12 o'clock midnight. Thus 9 hours and 50 minutes had already passed on 21 April '35.

The period of Venus is 20 years which is for 24 hours for the date 21. Thus, if 20 years are to be accounted in 24 hours, then what time of the main-period has elapsed in 9 hours 50 minutes?

On calculation, it will be seen that 1 hour is represented by 10 months and 1 minute by 5 days. Likewise, on calculation, 9 hours and 50 minutes represent 8 years 2 months and 10 days which is the period already elapsed in the main-period of Venus and the remainder is 11 years 9 months 20 days. Thus, a person born on 21-4-35 was in the main-period of Venus upto 11-2-47 and afterwards the main-period of Sun started.

While calculating the main-period, the planets are considered in the following manner or order:

Planet	Number	Duration of main-period in years
Venus	6	20
Sun	1	6
Moon	2	10
Mars	9	7
Rahu	4	18
Jupiter	3	16
Saturn	8	19
Mercury	5	17
Ketu	7	7

Thus, the period of Sun started on 11-2-47 whose period is 6 years and lasted till 11-2-53. Up to 11-2-63 there was the period of Moon and up to 11-2-70 the period of Mars. Up to 11-2-88 the period of Rahu would continue.

Sub-period

In the main-period (or generally called only period) of each planet, there are sub-periods of each planet. For the convenience of readers, I give below the tables of sub-periods:

Sub-period of Sun

		Year	Months	Days
Sun in	Sun	0	3	18
	Moon	0	6	0
	Mars	0	4	6
	Rahu	0	10	24
	Jupiter	0	9	18
	Saturn	0	11	12
	Mercury	0	10	6
	Ketu	0	4	6
	Venus	1	0	0

Sub-period of Moon

		Year	Months	Days
Moon in	Moon	0	10	0
	Mars	0	7	0
	Rahu	1	6	0
	Jupiter	1	4	0
	Saturn	1	7	0
	Mercury	1	5	0
	Ketu	0	7	0
	Venus	1	8	0
	Sun	0	6	0

Sub-period of Mars

		Year	Months	Days
Mars in	Mars	0	4	27
	Rahu	1	0	18
	Jupiter	0	11	6
	Saturn	1	0	9
	Mercury	0	11	27
	Ketu	0	4	27
	Venus	1	2	0
	Sun	0	4	6
	Moon	0	7	0

Sub-period of Rahu

		Year	Months	Days
Rahu in	Rahu	2	8	12
	Jupiter	2	4	14
	Saturn	2	10	6
	Mercury	2	6	18
	Ketu	1	0	18
	Venus	3	0	0
	Sun	0	10	24
	Moon	1	6	0
	Mars	1	0	18

Sub-period of Jupiter

	Year	Months	Days
Jupiter in Jupiter	2	1	18
Saturn	2	6	12
Mercury	2	3	6
Ketu	0	11	6
Venus	2	8	0
Sun	0	9	18
Moon	1	4	0
Mars	0	11	6
Rahu	2	4	24

Sub-period of Saturn

		Year	Months	Days
Saturn in	Saturn	3	0	3
	Mercury	2	8	9
	Ketu	1	1	9
	Venus	3	2	0
	Sun	0	11	12
	Moon	1	7	0
	Mars	1	1	9
	Rahu	2	10	6
	Jupiter	2	6	12

Sub-period of Mercury

		Year	Months	Days
Mercury in	Mercury	2	4	27
	Ketu	0	11	27
	Venus	2	10	0
	Sun	0	10	6
	Moon	1	5	0
	Mars	0	11	27
	Rahu	2	6	18
	Jupiter	2	3	6
	Saturn	2	8	9

Sub-period of Ketu

		Year	Months	Days
Ketu in	Ketu	0	4	27
	Venus	1	2	0
	Sun	0	4	6
	Moon	0	7	0
	Mars	0	4	27
	Rahu	1	0	18
	Jupiter	0	11	6
	Saturn	1	1	9
	Mercury	0	11	27

The sub-periods of all the nine planets have been made clear. In the example given on pg 85, the period of Rahu started from 11-2-70. Seeing the table, it is noted that the sub-period of Rahu in the main-period of Rahu is 2 years, 8 months and 12 days. Thus, the sub-period of Rahu was up to 23-10-72. After that the sub-period of Jupiter (see table on pg. 86) in the main period of Rahu is 2 years, 4 months and 24 days

Sub-period of Venus

		Year	Months	Days
Venus in	Venus	3	4	0
	Sun	1	0	0
	Moon	1	8	0
	Mars	1	2	0
	Rahu	3	0	0
	Jupiter	2	8	0
	Saturn	3	2	0
	Mercury	2	10	0
	Ketu	1	2	0

The sub-periods of all the nine planets have been made clear. In the example given on pg 85, the period of Rahu started from 11-2-70. Seeing the table, it is noted that the sub-period of Rahu in the main-period of Rahu is 2 years, 8 months and 12 days. Thus, the sub-period of Rahu was up to 23-10-72. After that the sub-period of Jupiter (see table on pg. 86) in the main period of Rahu is 2 years, 4 months and 24 days which will last up to 17-3-75. Likewise, the sub-period should be made clear.

Sub-sub-period

The division of a sub-period is called a sub-sub-period. To find the sub-sub-period, the years of the period of the main planet should be multiplied by the years of the planet of the sub-period. This multiplication should be multiplied by the years of the planet of the sub-sub-period and divide this number by 40. So the remainder will give the number of days of the sub-sub-period.

Example

Let us calculate the sub-sub-period of Moon in the sub-period of Moon in the main-period of Sun. Multiply the main-period of Sun which is 6 years with the main period of Moon which is 10 years, and we get 60 and in this the sub-sub-period of Moon is to be calculated. Thus, by multiplying 60 with the main-period of Moon which is 10 years, we will get 600. Dividing it by 40, we will get 15. Thus, the sub-sub-period of Moon in the sub-period of Moon in the main-period of Sun is 15 days. Likewise any other sub-sub-period can be calculated.

Prediction

The date of birth in the previous example is 21-4-35. The sum total is 15 = 6 which is represented by Venus.

In the above example, the sub-period of Saturn in the main-period of Rahu will start from 17-3-75. Number 4 is represented by Rahu and number 8 by Saturn. Both these numbers are inimical to number 6. Thus, the sub-period of Saturn will be harmful for it.

Similarly, the predictions for other periods should be understood. Predictions have been given in the previous chapter.

6
Yearly Predictions

With the help of numbers, a study of yearly predictions can be undertaken. What the effect of a particular number will be on a particular year and its result are explained below:

Method of marking the yearly predictions

1   Your birth date (number)

2   Number of the month

3   Year (in the year only last two digits should be written; for example, the year 1975 is written as 75)

4   Number of the day.

After totalling them up find the root number, which will represent the number of that year.

Let us take the previous example of the person who was born on 21-4-35. For him, the new year will start on 21-4-75.

1	Birth date	21
2	Month of birth	04
3	Present year	75
4	Day on 21-4-75 is Monday	02
	Total	102

Root number of 102 = 1 + 0 + 2 = 3

Thus, from 21-4-75 to 20-4-76, the number of year for this person will be 3.

For the convenience of readers, I give below the number of each day:

Sunday	1
Monday	2
Tuesday	9
Wednesday	5
Thursday	3
Friday	6
Saturday	8

Predictions

Whatever the number or digit, its effect will be as follows:

If the number for the year is 1

A most important year for you. In a few days, you will experience that all your problems prevailing for sometime past are being solved. You will feel healthier and the time will be favourable which will elate you.

You should plan things and try to do them. A new business or new work will be fruitful for you. In the coming days, you will yourself notice the important and favourable change which will be helpful in your elevation. The new persons and new officials you are likely to meet in the coming days will contribute to your elevation.

Your mental attitude will be healthier and stable throughout the year. Any new work or business started by you in this year will be of much importance to you. You will achieve success in education, competition, arts, business, writing and research work, if undertaken during this year.

This is the year for the accomplishment of your

desire, which could not materialise in the past. This year is governed by planet Sun and the configuration of other planets is favourable which will bring happy news for you and your position in society will be elevated with respect.

If the number for the year is 2

This year will be a very fascinating year for you. In the beginning of the year you are likely to come in contact with new faces who will prove helpful to you in your progress. The coming days and months will prove helpful and you will notice that all your plans are being executed favourably.

You are advised to remain cautious from deals having elements of a partnership in them this year as you are likely to lose in the game. You should not plump for cheap emotionalism or popularity. Be prudent in doing any work. Do not take any decision in haste.

This year you will be free from obstacles and problems which had plagued you in the past. Your strength and courage will be augmented. You will make yourself more stable by setting aside all imaginary thinking.

You should not lose contact with your friends as

they may be helpful in your life. But you should not hesitate to leave the company of those friends who have proved selfish.

You will gain from property matters during the year. Construction of a new house is contemplated. You will enjoy sound health this year.

If the number for the year is 3

This digit is an indication of wisdom, prestige and success. This year is definitely a year of prosperity for you. All the tasks which you could not complete earlier will be completed. You feel more satisfied and your monetary condition will improve substantially.

Your position in society will be augmented. You will have a feel of your personality. There will be an increase in your friends' circle. Momentary disappointments will change into new hopes.

Success in writing work is assured, if undertaken in this year. A favourable year for examinations, competitions and promotions. It is a year of success and full advantage must be taken of it.

This year will be favourable from the diplomatic and financial points of view. Control is desired in saying or writing anything to somebody. Great care may be taken before signing any paper as circumstances are not favourable and you may get deceived.

If the number for the year is 4

This year is a year of success. However, you will have to encounter a lot of problems before you accomplish your plans or aims. The year is an indicator for you to become active. The harder you work, the greater the gains in this year.

The year will make you more stable financially. Your means of income will be augmented. You will become more self-dependent and your savings will be more with which you can multiply your wealth. Buying of a new house or starting a new business is indicated in this year.

A good year for marriage. In case you are unmarried, there is an indication of your getting a spouse. If already married, there is a possibility of being blessed with a child in this year. Your hurdles diminish and auspicious work in your house will start. You are likely to experience more happiness from your friends, spouse and children. Romance and love will be normal in this year.

You are likely to develop intimate, friendly relations

with high officials, and thereby achieve benefits. This is a most favourable year from the point of view of spiritual, religious and foreign visits.

If the number for the year is 5

This year is governed by the influence of the planet Mercury which represents gentleness and wisdom, and is a year of success. This year will take a favourable turn and your prestige and position in society will be enhanced.

Travelling is indicated this year, for amusement or for business. Foreign travel is likely. If a new business is started with a partnership, it will be fruitful.

You must exercise control on your tongue. You must take due care and precaution before signing any papers. If you are engaged in education, competition, drama, radio, communication, publicity, telephone, telegraph or postal services, this will be an epoch-making year for you.

This year will be favourable and beneficial from the business point of view. The more you work, the more gains you will have. Expand your business and undertake such jobs as will improve your financial condition.

If appearing in any examination, or in a competition this year, you will positively succeed. Better health, financial stability, defeat of enemies, increase in the number of friends, completion of jobs are indicated in this year. This will be a memorable year of your life.

If the number for the year is 6

A most important year from the point of view of the family-and-home front. You will notice that the worries which had engulfed you have vanished and you will experience more peace, contentment and happiness.

Family problems will be over at the commencement of the year. There is a likelihood of your being blessed with a child. You will partake of love and romance and there is no possibility of getting defamed or being entangled in difficulties.

You will spend on amusement, decoration and articles concerning beauty. You are likely to buy a new television or any other new instrument for entertainment. You will be much benefited if you do a job related to cinema. To those who are already in the cinema line, this year will prove most progressive and prosperous.

You can gain much from trade on articles concerning beauty. New acquaintances and new friendships will be established and prove beneficial. In case you are unemployed, you will get employment. Financially it is a good year.

A favourable year from the educational point of view. Transfer to a desired place or promotion of persons who are in education is indicated this year. Success is indicated in competitions.

New business will start. There is a possibility of your making sudden financial gains through a lady. Success in the philosophical field, too. All your physical desires will be fulfilled.

If the number for the year is 7

This digit represents problems and suspicion. You will notice that at the beginning of the year, environments will take such shape that they will be looked upon with a suspicious mind in society. Therefore, in the beginning of the year, you must take care and see that you do not take actions that create doubts in people's minds.

Mental worries will increase. You will notice that your friends for whom you had sacrificed are creating problems for you. You must remain alert and screen your friends to determine who are favourable and who are not.

Success in business is indicated though it may be attended by obstacles. During the start of the year some problems will be there, but there is nothing to get disheartened or disgruntled over. Difficulties will vanish and you will experience favourable conditions. Harder you work, greater the gains.

Possibility of getting defamed in this year exists. You will have to be cautious in romance. You must take all precautions in doing any work so that it may not create any troubles for you. Do not take much risk in business. Do not entangle yourself in arguments and quarrels with anyone.

Undoubtedly, you are going to win litigation or any other matter pending in law courts.

It is a year of success in science, medical treatment, magic, astrology, medical sciences, etc. Your prestige and position in society will go up. You will experience that people will look at you with respect. Financially, it is a sound year.

If the number for the year is 8

If you utilize your energy in the right way, undoubtedly this year will prove beneficial and successful.

You may be affected by blood pressure, heart attack, blood shortage, etc., and you are advised to take due care in this regard.

A very fruitful year for business enterprises. If business is started or expanded this year, progress will be astonishing. Business relating to machinery or iron will be more profitable. This year will be favourable for those who are in Government service, as they will either get a promotion or more facilities. Socially this is a bright year. From the political point of view, this is a favourable year. You will shortly be extricated from problems which had entangled you. You will feel healthier and experience more stability.

Your enemies will be defeated. You will win cases in law courts. Business will prosper. Side business with partnership will start which will prove beneficial later. An important year as far as freedom is concerned. Your family relations will be favourable. A foreign tour is indicated. You will dominate your enemies throughout the year.

Progress in this year will be due to your own efforts.

Very little contribution to your progress may be there from others. Towards the end of the year, you will feel satisfied with the progress made.

If the number for the year is 9

This is a lucky and important year for you. If you appear for an examination, you will succeed. Also significant from the financial angle, you may get a windfall. Business expansion will be successful. You will occupy an important position in society. Wishes will be fulfilled and auspicious things will occur at home.

You will succeed in spiritual endeavour and attain a high position in education, examination, research and business.

If in service, you will progress steadily. Though you will have differences of opinion with your superiors, they will not have any adverse effect on your career. You should give up your old ways and adjust to new methods. If you mix more with the people around, you will gain in self-confidence, happiness, love and money.

Whichever number works out for the year, the period of that number starts first. In the previous example, the number of the year was 3. Thus, the period of number 3 or Jupiter will start first. I explain below the number and its period:

Number	Planet	Period	
		Months	Days
1	Sun	0	18
2	Moon	1	00
9	Mars	0	21
4	Rahu	1	24
3	Jupiter	1	18
8	Saturn	1	27
5	Mercury	1	21
7	Ketu	0	21
6	Venus	2	00

In the example cited, after making clear the period for the year 1975, the following table will be made:

Number	Period		From	To
	Months	Days		
3	1	18	21-4-75	9-6-75
8	1	27	9-6-75	6-8-75
5	1	21	6-8-75	27-9-75
7	0	21	27-9-75	18-10-75
6	2	00	18-10-75	18-12-75
1	0	18	18-12-75	6-1-76
2	1	00	6-1-76	6-2-76
9	0	21	6-2-76	27-2-76
4	1	24	27-2-76	21-4-76

On 21-4-76, a new year will start for this person.

Predictions

Predictions should be made keeping in view the relationship between the number of the year and the number of the period. In the previous chapter, the relationship between various numbers and their results were indicated. Keeping that in view, predictions should be made.

7
Monthly Predictions

Monthly predictions can be calculated in a way similar to the way the yearly predictions are calculated.

1 Present month

2 Present year

3 Birth date

4 Year of birth

5 Number of months from the last birth date.

Adding them up, find the root number which will be the number of the month.

A new month will be counted from birth date to birth date. In the previous example, the date of birth of the person is 21-4-35. Thus the new month will run from the 21st to the 20th of the following month.

Let us take the previous example. The man's date of birth is 21-4-35 and we have to find out the number of July 1975.

1	Present month — July	:	07
2	Present year	:	75
3	Birth date	:	21
4	Year of birth	:	35
5	Number of months from 21-4-35 to 20-7-75	:	03
	Total		141

Root number of 141 = 1 + 4 + 1 = 6

Thus in this example, the number of the month from 21-7-75 to 20-8-75 is 6 whose planet is Venus.

Predictions

If the number for the month is 1

A favourable month. Some new work will start and

your social status will increase. You will be able to solve problems which had been pending for sometime. Your enemies will be defeated and you will experience a better state of mind and body. You will come into contact with prominent persons and this will prove beneficial to you later. You will gain more from dealings concerning advertisements and iron. A favourable month for those who are in service. You will experience more happiness.

If the number for the month is 2

A favourable month, undoubtedly. You should march ahead with someone's help. You will notice that in this period you are financially much better off. Your success in romance and conversion of your money into wealth are certain to materialise.

If you do not take precaution, trouble may break out on your family front which may cause unnecessary embarrassment to you. You should avoid getting angry.

To remain in an imaginary world is not favourable to you. You are likely to be deceived in this month. A confidence-inspiring friend may even try to cheat you. There are travels in this month for you which will prove beneficial financially. You should not indulge in uphill tasks. Never undertake any work which may create problems for you later.

If the number for the month is 3

A favourable month from all points of view. A little effort will bring success. All your pending jobs will be accomplished. You will experience happiness, gains and success.

You are required to keep yourself busy throughout this month. Every moment is valuable. You are going to win laurels from plans made in this month. You are cautioned not to enter into any big deal or invest your income in this month.

Success in business is not ruled out. New works will commence. New contacts with high-ups will be established. Sources of income will increase. If in service, your work for which you had been making concerted efforts for sometime past, will be completed.

If the number for the month is 4

You are likely to face obstacles this month. You will notice that greater the efforts you make, greater the hurdles you encounter. My advice is that you should not get disappointed or disgruntled. This is a temporary phase and you will triumph over it and even benefit from it. As a matter of fact, this is the end of the period of obstructions. In this month, whatever work you start or whatever decision you take, you start reaping fruits in the coming months.

Do not have blind faith in anybody. A possibility of financial loss is there. Whatever work you undertake, do it in a systematic way. Take all precautions before signing any papers. Do not make haste in taking decisions in this month.

Obstacles and hurdles in service are only to be expected. You may indulge in arguments with high officials. Laxity in romance is expected and if planning fails, the chances of getting defamed cannot be ruled out.

If the number for the month is 5

This month represents changes. In this period all your work will be accomplished for which you had been anxiously waiting for sometime past. You should take full advantage of this month and whatever work you undertake, try to complete it as early as possible.

A favourable month from the business point of view. New work will commence which will bring profits to you. Financially, an excellent month for you.

A favourable month for examination, competition, research, knowledge, writing, music, drawing, painting, which will ensure success for you.

You are advised to have perseverance and never make haste. To take advice from others may ultimately prove beneficial. This month indicates success in service.

If the number for the month is 6

A favourable month from the economic and educational points of view. It also indicates that the obstacles which had come in the last month will be over and happiness will prevail.

Love and romance will prosper. Financial gains from a lady are indicated. Married life will become congenial and you will be able to discharge your responsibilities satisfactorily. Thus, this month is prosperous on all fronts.

To those persons who are associated with art or films, this month will be most rewarding. You will be able to fulfil your desires and attain a respectable position in society.

If the number for the month is 7

In this month, you will face obstacles and difficulties. The more you try to get extricated from them, the more intractable the problems will be. You should tackle problems with perseverance and calm. Take decisions yourself and avoid work which may create problems for you.

You will feel irritated in family life. You will not be fully successful in business. A word of caution — no laxity in business. Otherwise it may create problems for you. The more efforts you put in, the more success you attain.

If the number for the month is 8

This month indicates weak health. But you will experience that all the obstacles which used to worry you in the past are over and you will feel fresh and cheerful. A most lucky month for you. Success is assured in business. A little effort augments business. If you initiate any new work in this month, success is certain.

A most favourable month economically. New sources of income will develop and your bank balance will increase. You will get help from friends and colleagues. Those in service will achieve success and fulfil their ambitions. Likely to be defamed in romance: you should be cautious. This month is favourable all over.

If the number for the month is 9

Number 9 is an indication of tremendous progress and splendid success. You should take full advantage of this month. Each minute of the month is very valuable and useful. You will gain in honour and respect.

New sources of income will develop and you will achieve complete success in business. If you are already in business, you will notice that all the problems which worried you earlier are being resolved.

From the service point of view, this is a successful month. You will get promotion, financial gains and happiness. Your relations with officials will be cordial and you can take advantage of them.

Period of months

Number	Planet	Period
1	Sun	2
2	Moon	3
9	Mars	2
4	Rahu	4
3	Jupiter	4
8	Saturn	5
5	Mercury	4
7	Ketu	2
6	Venus	4

Whatever the number of the month, that month's period will start first in the above order.

In the previous example, the number of the month is 6. Therefore, first the period of number 6 will start and then of 1, 2, 9, 4, 3, 8, 5 and 7.

In the previous example, the new year started on 21-7-75. The month-wise period will be as given below:

Number	Planet	Period	From	To
6	Venus	4	21-7-75	24-7-75
1	Sun	2	25-7-75	26-7-75
2	Moon	3	27-7-75	29-7-75
9	Mars	2	30-7-75	31-7-75
4	Rahu	4	1-8-75	4-8-75
3	Jupiter	4	5-8-75	8-8-75
8	Saturn	5	9-8-75	13-8-75
5	Mercury	4	14-8-75	17-8-75
7	Ketu	2	18-8-75	20-8-75

If the month has 30 or 31 days and whatever period is left either less or more can be subtracted from or added to the past period. Thus in this month, the individual has to undergo the period of Ketu for 3 days instead of 2 days.

Predictions should be based on the relationship between the month-number and the period-number, as indicated in the last chapter.

8
Daily Predictions

Daily predictions can also be calculated on the lines
of monthly predictions.

1   Year of birth

2   Month of birth

3   Date of birth

4   Present month

5   Present date

6   Present day

Add them up and then find the root number.
The number you get is the number of the day.

Let us apply it to the previous example. Suppose today is 17 February, 1975:

Year of birth	35
Month of birth	04 (April)
Date of birth	21
Present year	75
Present month	02 (February)
Present date	17
Present day	02 (Tuesday)
Total	156

The root number is $1 + 5 + 6 = 12 = 1 + 2 = 3$

Thus, the root number of 17-2-1975 is 3, which is governed by planet Jupiter.

Predictions

If the number for the day is 1

On this day you will achieve success. Financial gains are expected. Relations with new acquaintances will be established and they will contribute to your progress in life.

If the number for the day is 2

You are likely to be deceived. Exercise due care and caution while undertaking any work or signing any papers. Favourable from the monetary point of view.

If the number for the day is 3

A progressive day. Very little efforts will bring quite gainful results. Officials will help you. Business will prosper and you will command respect from society.

If the number for the day is 4

You will succeed after overcoming some problems. You should not get disappointed. Before the sun sets, you will achieve success.

If the number for the day is 5

A day of complete success. Success in an examination or a competition. Achievement of aims will be made easy. From the business and monetary points of view, it is a favourable day.

If the number for the day is 6

Success in love and romance. Sudden financial gains. Business will prosper. Relations with new acquaintances will be established and your desires fulfilled.

If the number for the day is 7

Unnecessary obstacles and worries will be there. The more the efforts you put in to make your going easy, the more difficult the problems become. A day of failures and mental agonies.

If the number for the day is 8

Complete success. All your efforts will be rewarded. Relations with new acquaintances will be established. Little efforts go a long way.

If the number for the day is 9

Lucky day. Unaccounted gains, success and victory are the highlights. All the problems which you had been facing for sometime past will be resolved. A happy and cheerful day.

Hourly predictions

Now for the benefit of readers, I am giving the ruling number for each hour for all the 24 hours of the day and night.

In the table overleaf, the time reference should be taken from 12 noon. For example, if you want to know what will be the ruling number of Monday at 3 p.m., see in the row of 3 and in the column of Monday and we get the number 7, which is the number of Ketu. Therefore, on Monday between 3 p.m. and 4 p.m. the ruling effective number will be 8. Similarly, other days can also be studied.

Hour Table

Time	Sun	Mon	Tues	Wed	Thurs	Fri	Sat
Noon	2	5	9	1	6	3	7
1	7	6	1	3	3	2	2
2	6	1	6	4	4	4	8
3	8	7	5	8	9	5	9
4	9	8	7	5	8	9	5
5	4	4	8	6	1	6	4
6	1	3	3	2	2	7	6
7	2	5	9	1	6	3	7
8	7	6	1	3	3	2	2
9	6	1	6	4	4	4	8
10	8	7	5	8	9	5	9
11	9	8	7	5	8	9	5
12	4	4	8	6	1	6	4
13	1	3	3	2	2	7	6
14	2	5	9	1	6	3	7
15	7	6	1	3	3	2	

Time	Sun	Mon	Tues	Wed	Thurs	Fri	Sat
16	6	1	6	4	4		
17	8	7	5	8	9		
18	9	8	7	5	8		
19	4	4	8	6	1		
20	1	3	3	2	2		
21	2	5	9	1			
22	7	6	1	3			
23	6	1	6	4			

In case we want to go into precise details, the following table will be helpful wherein the difference of 4-4 minutes has been explained. From top to bottom, minutes have been indicated and from left to right, it represents days. This is the end of the minute-period.

For example, if we want to find out which number or planet will have its effect at 18 minutes past 3 p.m., we have to make use of the table given overleaf. In the column for Monday, up to 16 minutes, number 9 is effective and afterwards up to 20 minutes, the number is 1. Thus that time was under the effect of number 1 or the planet Sun.

Minute Table

Minutes	Sun	Mon	Tues	Wed	Thurs	Fri	Sat
4	1	7	9	5	3	6	8
8	6	8	1	7	9	5	3
12	5	3	6	8	1	7	9
16	7	9	5	3	6	8	1
20	8	1	7	9	5	3	6
24	3	6	8	1	7	9	5
28	9	5	3	6	8	1	7
32	1	7	9	5	3	6	8
36	6	8	1	7	9	5	3
40	5	3	6	8	1	7	9
44	7	9	5	3	6	8	1
48	8	1	7	9	5	3	6
52	3	6	8	1	7	9	5
56	9	5	3	6	8	1	7
60	1	7	9	5	3	6	8

Likewise, the day number of 17-2-75 is 3 and at 18 minutes past 3, the Sun or number 1 was effective.

The numbers with their effects which have been described in the last chapter may be studied.

It may be seen that on Monday, 17-2-75, between 3 and 4, number 7 was effective and between 16 and 20 minutes, number 1 was effective.

The calculations are as follows:

Day number   3

Hour number   7

Minute number   1

Total   11

The root number is 1 + 1 = 2

Number 2 represents the Moon which aspects favourably the planet Venus of a person born on 21-4-35. Thus, whatever decision he will take will be favourable and gainful.

I will explain on the following page the effect of the hour-number and the minute-number:

If it is a hour number

1 — indicates success

2 — success with little obstruction

3 — full gains

4 — problems and failures

5 — full gains

6 — happiness and favourable conditions

7 — deceit, problems and failures

8 — gainful prospects

9 — most lucky outlook

If it is a minute number

1 — indicates success

2 — success with obstructions

3 — gainful prospects

4 — failures

5 — gainful outlook

6 — gains, happiness and progress

7 — failures

8 — gainful possibility

9 — coupled with special luck

9
Name and Number

A name has significance. Man is recognised by his name and as such his aim, target, efforts are only intended to glorify his name. His efforts are directed towards more and more people knowing him and he attains a high position in society.

Western numerologists have given a thought to this. They have fixed a number that represents a particular letter and the sum of all such numbers corresponding to each letter of one's name indicates one's worth. Well-known Western numerologist, Cheiro, has fixed the following number corresponding to each letter of the English alphabet:

Letter	Number
A	1
B	2
C	3
D	4
E	5
F	8
G	3
H	5
I	1
J	1
K	2
L	3
M	4
N	5
O	7
P	8
Q	1
R	2

Letter	Number
S	3
T	4
U	6
V	6
W	6
X	5
Y	1
Z	7

Knowing the number for a particular letter, the name of a person can easily be converted into numbers. For example, the name of INDIRA GANDHI can be converted into numbers as shown below:

Letter	Number
I	1
N	5
D	4
I	1

Letter	Number
R	2
A	1
G	3
A	1
N	5
D	4
H	5
I	1

The sum-total is 33. Likewise, we can convert the name of any town, person, association, country or our own officer and know whether it will be in our favour or not.

The meaning of the single numbers from 1 to 9 represents how the person appears in the eyes of his followers. They are numbers of individuality and personality. All numbers from 10 up become 'double' or 'compound' numbers.

According to numerology, compound numbers have their own peculiarity. I am mentioning below the effect of such compound numbers from which one can know good or bad, loss or gain. From these facts, the following queries can be answered:

1 Will it be helpful for augmenting my personality?

2 By making a little change in my name, can I make things favourable and rise in life?

3 Is the compound number of my name favourable to my date of birth?

4 Is the city or town where I presently live favourable for my betterment?

5 Is the name of my wife (or husband) favourable to me or not?

6 Is there synchronisation in the compound number of my name and my partners?

7 Is the firm or factory with which I am associated favourable?

8 Is the compound number of the name of my son or daughter favourable to the date of birth?

9 Is the compound number of my name favourable or associated with the compound numbers of the names of my children.

Similar questions are always a matter of concern

to a person for which he wants solutions. Some change in the name is helpful in such situations.

The effect of numbers from 1 to 9 has been given earlier and now I proceed to give the effect of compound numbers which belong more to the spiritual side of life.

10   It is a number of will power, perseverance, faith and self-confidence. Once these persons determine to undertake a job, they do not rest till it is completed. Though born in ordinary families, they attain high positions in life.

11   Symbolises a person with a weak and unstable mind. Such persons make efforts to progress but are disappointed soon. They achieve success with great difficulty.

12   It indicates sacrifice. Friends, colleagues and relatives will continuously take advantage of them and will deceive them. Such persons have continuous suffering and anxiety of mind.

13   This is a number indicating change of plans. Persons start work with zest and enthusiasm but soon become indolent. Generally they are found unsuccessful.

14   Such persons are lucky. Sudden gains come in their life many times. With their own efforts, they

succeed in their aims. They are sociable and fortunate.

15   This number represents mystery. Such persons take interest in occult sciences and music. Most of the time of their life is spent in these activities. What is in their mind is not reflected on their face and as such it is very difficult to understand them. This number symbolises luck, courage and sustainable progress.

16   Such persons are under the continuous grip of uncertainty. Sudden incidents take place in their life. They rise quickly and fall with the same alacrity. Such persons have continuously to face fatalities of some sort or the other.

17   Such persons rise superior to the trials and difficulties in their lives. They do not rest till they achieve their goals. They are broad-minded and possess the qualities of perseverance and forgiveness. They are honoured for their deeds.

18   This number is an indicator of opposition and failure. Such persons are always gripped by problems and mental agonies. This is not a favourable number from the family point of view.

19   This number is considered to be that of a lover of justice. Such persons become famous throughout their life for this. They are civilised and disciplined.

20 This symbolises the prosperity of a person. Persons born in humble circumstances achieve high positions in life. There is no dearth of honour and respect for them.

21 This number represents a most favourable time and success. Such persons continue to progress. They are noted for their integrity. In whatever field they are, they are capable of fulfilling their desires and attaining their aims.

22 This digit represents emotion. Such persons live in an imaginary world. They cannot see anybody in distress and are ready to help them. They even go to any length to sacrifice for them. They cannot face the struggles of life. Numerologists have rightly named them as dreamers.

23 Such people can take neither any initiative nor quick decisions. They work according to the advice of their friends or acquaintances. They continuously face obstructions, a fact that hampers their progress.

24 This number is lucky, Such people work according to their scheduled plan and do not allow laxity in it. They have a leaning towards the opposite sex.

25 This number brings mixed gains. They do succeed but after surmounting obstacles and problems. Though they are hard-working, adopt new ideas and march forward, they do not achieve complete success due to obstructions.

26   Such persons are very clever and keep a hawk's eye on their profits. They cannot be relied upon easily. Anytime they can deceive others.

27   Such persons are intelligent, clever and are quick in their work. By their prudence, they attain their goals and an honourable position in society. Their ideas are original and nascent. They are counted among the successful personalities in their circle.

28   This number is full of contradictions. It has as good an effect as a bad one. Such persons are very hardworking, have perseverance and are alert but they are not successful. Problems are always dominant in their life.

29   This number indicates uncertainty. They think a thousand times before undertaking any work, yet they are unable to make a beginning with it. In case they initiate any work, they cannot complete it. They waste money and time on false prestige and show.

30   This is a number of thoughtful deduction and retrospection. Their position in society is due to their mental superiority and greatness. They have confidence in their wisdom and rise in life. They attach more importance to education than to materialistic things.

31   This number represent largely self-contained

persons. They are lonely and isolated from their fellows. It is not a fortunate number from the materialistic point of view.

32 These persons are successful, subtle and progressive due to their intelligence. If they undertake any work seriously, they can accomplish it. Laziness is their weakness.

33 This number is an indicator of self-confidence. Whatever work they undertake, they do not stop till they complete it. They have unlimited patience, unshattering self-confidence and strong vigour which are their characteristics. They succeed fully in life.

34 Such persons have to face many problems. They often entertain reservations in their mind due to which they do not and cannot impress others. They cannot dare to talk to high officials. Due to their inferiority complex, they do not succeed in life.

35 Such persons believe in living by hook or crook. They neither have any desire for new work nor do they make any effort to rise in life. They shift responsibility to others and manage to remain carefree.

36 Such persons stick to their words and are highly respected. They carry out the delegated responsibility and then pause. They are successful in their aims. They are mature and adopt the right path.

37 This number represents help and assistance. Success for persons with this number is only possible when they work either with somebody or with somebody's help. They are most circumspect and careful as far as their intelligence and prestige are concerned.

38 This number indicates instability. Such persons cannot stick to one place, cannot think for long on a particular subject. They are more successful in field work.

39 This number stands for courage and boldness. Such people have a fertile brain. They never get disheartened or disgruntled with hurdles which come in their way but march on. Their efforts are finally successful and fruitful.

40 Such people are atheistic outwardly, they are inwardly God-fearing and religious-minded.

41 Such persons though born in ordinary families rise to high positions. By making efforts, they realise their aims in life. Their intelligence is praiseworthy. They are honoured and respected in society.

42 Such persons are parasites. Though they have wisdom and merit, they are unable to utilise them fruitfully. They rise in life with others' assistance.

43 This number represents obstructions. Such persons are failures in their life. Often they are involved in

litigations, quarrels and intractable problems.

44 They can't work without others' help. This becomes clear when they seek others' help and get deceived or suffer or create unnecessary problems for themselves and others.

45 Such persons have high ambitions and aspirations in life and get completely merged in them. They are capable of moulding themselves to a given environment. They are successful in achieving their ambitions.

46 This is a lucky number. Unexpected events take place in their lives, sometimes, very abruptly. Whatever work they undertake, they do it in a unique way which is worth praising widely in society.

47 This number represents uncertainty. Nothing can be definitely predicted about any incident in their lives. Though possessed of high calibre, such persons lead a poor, uneventful and simple life.

48 This number indicates wisdom, merit and simplicity. Such people remain simple in life but are a gift to society and are remembered with reverence for a long time to come.

49 Such persons are self-sufficient. They are easily defeated in their social struggles. They are rarely seen in society and have few friends.

50 This number represents a fertile imagination. Such persons are emotionally surcharged, helpful and kind. They are far removed from the realities of life. They are always under constant stress and strain. They are of a dreamy nature and love to dream.

51 This number represents complete victory. Struggles are rare in life. But when they are obliged to struggle, they become more active and alert. They have quite a few enemies but are not harmed by them.

52 This number symbolises defeat and problems. Such people do not have an easy time. Their life is clouded in turbulence and troubles with problems.

53 This number represents secrecy. Such persons do not reveal their plans. Nothing can be predicted or read from their face about what is on their mind. Despite ups and downs, their facial expression remains unchanged. This quality makes them successful. They make good social or political spies.

54 This number points to leadership. Such people are capable of providing leadership to society and country. With their leadership, swift decisions and wisdom, they achieve their aims quickly.

55 This number represents hoary wisdom. These people are good orators and defeat their opponents by their

arguments. They do not pause till they win respect and honour with their own efforts.

56 This is a number that represents obstacles. Although such persons want to rise in life, they do not succeed, due to their faulty planning. They have friends who are weak and without foresight.

57 This number points to self-confidence, and spreading happiness. Such people are most successful in their business or occupation. Their only aim in life is to march ahead.

58 Life is frank and truthful like an open book. They entertain neither any malice nor contemplate any low deed. On the whole, they are fully successful in their life.

59 Such persons have to face many upheavals in life. They are flexible in their character. Their main aim is to get money by hook or crook. They manage to be economically stable in the long run.

60 A mark of people with this number is to remain always cheerful and make others happy. They exude sunshine. They never feel disheartened or discouraged even under difficult circumstances. They are successful in medical practice, and in tasks related to social service and welfare.

61 They practice self-control and are men of few words.

Initially, they have to face a lot of problems but soon they get over them and succeed.

62   This number indicates complete success in military leadership. Such persons act fast and possess great self-confidence with which they achieve success.

63   This number represents welfare. To help others and keep busy in religious matters is their trait. They command full respect in society.

64   This number indicates mental agonies and instability in life. Family life is not happy.

65   This number represents accidents. Some incident or other inevitably takes place in their life. Their whole life is an unmitigated saga of struggles and strains.

66   This number stands for success. Such persons attain full success in whatever they attempt and whichever field they choose to work in and they are ever mindful of their goals.

67   Such persons are simple and good hearted. Socially, they are respected and honoured.

68   These persons are often nervous and worried. Their life is full of turbulence and ups and downs. This number represents fraud, deceit and such other evils.

69   This number symbolises fame. These persons win wealth. They are very happy, contented and revered widely.

70   This is indeed a lucky number. They succeed in whatever field they are in. Their old age is very happy, peaceful and contented.

71   A number which represents obstacles. Such people are always confronted with problems due to which they cannot rest on their oars. They always entertain some sort of doubt in their minds. They are nicknamed 'doubting Thomases' in their social circles.

72   This number indicates hard work. Such persons succeed after surmounting lots of problems and overcoming hurdles. Even after hard labour, no sign of disappointment is visible on their faces.

73   This is an ordinary number. Such persons attain success with great exertion. They feel disappointed due to excessive obstacles. In their case, the game is not worth the candle.

74   This number indicates complete success and absolute superiority. Though born in ordinary circumstances, they rise in life by dint of their own efforts. They go on struggling and finally achieve success.

75 This number points towards luxury. Such people are wordly-minded, atheistic and want to lead a luxurious life. They always experience shortage of money.

76 This is an unfortunate number. Such persons do not succeed even after striving very hard. They are always struggling with some problem or the other.

77 This number represents attachment. Such men are extremely selfish. Before undertaking any work, they see their self-interest first. They are not socially respected or well-spoken of, even in their own intimate circles.

78 This number is an indicator of money. Opportunities for getting money knock on their door many times in their life. They succeed in tasks where others normally fail. They possess a business aptitude and exploit it fully.

79 This number indicates sacrifice. Such persons help others even at their own cost. In the public domain they are progressive and exert themselves for the common good.

80 Complete success is represented by this number. They rise in life due to their own efforts. From the four points of view of religion, wealth, love and renouncement, they are happy, contented and successful.

I have endeavoured to make clear the properties of various compound numbers. A person should strive to stabilize the compound number of his name which ensures progress in life. I am explaining it with an example below:

A person named Nand Kishor came to see me. He used to write his name as below with the compound number as:

N A N D K I S H O R

5 1 5 4 2 1 3 5 7 2

Total = 35

Compound number 35 does not have a good effect. If we go back a few pages and read the effect of the compound number 35, (see pg. 136) we shall notice that such people are not successful. After he came in my contact, I advised him to add letter 'A' at the end of KISHOR. Then the compound number of NAND KISHORA becomes 36 which is an indication of complete success. With this small alteration in his name he has since led a very successful life.

Readers are advised to make small changes in their names in order to obtain better results. Suppose a person's name is Rajinder Mal Bhandari, he can write it as R.M. Bhandari. Likewise, any addition to or subtraction from the surname can be made more gainful.

Readers are advised to make their compound numbers synchronous with the root number of their date of birth. For example, the number is 8 of a person born on 4-3-37. Suppose the sum total of the numbers allotted to the letters of his name comes to 37. This number reduces to $3 + 7 = 10 = 1 + 0 = 1$. Number 1 is inimical to number 8. Thus, the numbers of the date of birth and of the name clash with each other. Thus, readers should make changes in the letters of their names in such a way that the compound numbers derived from them are gainful. Secondly, the root number of the compound number should tally with the root number of the date of birth or view it in a friendly way.

A person cannot change his date of birth but can make changes in his name and make it favourable and achieve success in life.

Similarly, relations with partners, husband-wife relations, name related to industry/factory, son, etc., can be worked out.

Thus, with the use of numerology, we can solve many problems ourselves and thereby progress in life.

10
The Pyramid Method

By the pyramid method we can find answers to our questions.

In a question, firstly the number of words are written and then the letters in each word are written. For example, if a person asks, "Shall I pass in my examination?"

This sentence has 6 words. Thus, number 6 is written first. The 'shall' has 5 letters, 'I' has 1, 'pass' has 4, 'in' has 2, 'my' has 2, 'examination' has 11 letters. In case a word has more than 9 letters, then the root number should be written. Examination has 11 letters. Thus $1 + 1 = 2$ will be written. A question should not have more than 9 words.

The above question can be mentioned in numbers as follows:

6 5 1 4 2 2 2

The method of making a pyramid is to write the root number of the sum of the first and second numbers below them. Then the root numbers of the second and third numbers are written below them. Likewise, go on making a pyramid. The pyramid of the above figure will be as follows:

```
6 5 1 4 2 2 2
 2 6 5 6 4 4
  8 2 2 1 8
   1 4 3 9
    5 7 3
     3 1
      4
```

Thus, the pyramid number of the question is 4.

Now, I will explain below the effect of pyramid numbers:

If the number of the pyramid is 1

This number represents complete success. You are shortly going to meet a person who will be helpful to you and you will achieve success in the coming days.

If the number of the pyramid is 2

This number indicates uncertainty. Possibility of some obstructions. Success cannot be achieved even after making efforts.

If the number of the pyramid is 3

You will be making concerted efforts. In the near future, your expenses will increase. You will only be able to succeed in your goal with the help of someone. Your efforts will not go futile.

If the number of the pyramid is 4

You will have to face many more hurdles and obstructions in your work. The greater the efforts you make to overcome them, the more problems will be created. But success in work is definite.

If the number of the pyramid is 5

This number represents complete success through travels. You should either correspond with concerned officers or meet them personally. You should intensify your efforts and victory will be yours.

If the number of the pyramid is 6

Time is propitious. You will succeed in your aims with the help of a friend or a lady. Completion of work will bring happiness.

If the number of the pyramid is 7

This number indicates success in work. Although you have to face obstacles for sometime more, their end is in sight and you will achieve success. With the success in your work, you will be respected in society.

If the number of the pyramid is 8

Success in your work is uncertain. Your enemies are active and their efforts are stronger. A wrong impression about you has been formed with the result that your success is cast in doubt. Obstacles in your work, loss of money and problems cannot be ruled out.

If the number of the pyramid is 9

Shortly your enemies will be defeated and you will attain your goal. You will notice that all your problems which had plagued you thus far have vanished and you are marching swiftly to your objective. Success is before you and there is nothing to feel disheartened or disgruntled about.

Readers should now be able to find answers to their questions by this method.

Likewise you can find the pyramid number of your name and can use it in finding the relations of your partners and husband-wife relations. If the pyramid numbers of two persons are friendly, then they will remain friends throughout their lives. For example, if the pyramid number of a husband is 3 and that of a wife is 9. The numbers 3 and 9 are friends and thus both the husband and wife will have congenial relations. Similarly, from our pyramid number, we can find our relations with officers or a firm from their pyramid numbers. By changing the spellings of the name, the pyramid number can be made favourable to the pyramid number of others.

Y es, I would like to be a member of the

World Wisdom Book Club

Name ☐ Mr ☐ Mrs ☐ Ms ....

Mailing Address ....

....

....

City .... Pin ....

Phone .... Fax ....

E-mail ....

Profession .... D.O.B. ....

Areas of Interest ....

....

Mail this form to:
The World Wisdom Book Club
J-40, Jorbagh Lane, New Delhi 110003
Tel: 24620063, 55654197 • Fax: 24645795

NUMEROLOGY MADE EASY